The Golden Book
MONT-SAINT-MICHEL

Nicolas Simonnet
Curator of Mont-Saint-Michel

CONTENTS

Preface .... *Page* 3

THE BAY .... " 8
- The tides .... " 8
- Silting .... " 10
- The fauna .... " 12

THE CITY .... " 13
THE DEFENSES .... " 14
THE OLD HOUSES .... " 16
COMMERCE .... " 17
THE PARISH CHURCH .... " 18

THE ABBEY .... " 19
- The foundation of the abbey .... " 19
- The Carolingian church .... " 20
- The Benedictine abbey .... " 21
THE ABBEY CHURCH .... " 23
- The nave .... " 24
- The transept .... " 27
THE ROMANESQUE BUILDINGS OF THE CONVENT .... " 29
- The dormitory .... " 30
- The promenoir .... " 30
- The Crypte de l'Aquilon .... " 30
- Entrance to the Romanesque abbey .... " 31
ROBERT DE TORIGNY'S APARTMENTS .... " 32
- The porter's lodgings and the dungeons .... *Page* 32
- The Southern buildings .... " 33
- Chapelle Saint-Etienne .... " 33
- The ossuary and the large wheel .... " 33
- Monastic life .... " 35
THE MERVEILLE .... " 35
- The Eastern building of the Merveille .... " 38
- The Western building of the Merveille .... " 39
- The monks' refectory .... " 40
- The cloister .... " 42
- Salle des Hôtes .... " 46
- Salle des Chevaliers .... " 48
- The almonry .... " 50
- The cellar .... " 51
- The guard room .... " 52
BELLE-CHAISE AND THE ABBOT'S LODGINGS .... " 53
THE HUNDRED YEARS WAR .... " 54
THE FLAMBOYANT GOTHIC CHOIR .... " 55

THE MONT IN MODERN TIMES .... " 57
- The Mont, state prison .... " 58
- The restoration .... " 59

THE RAMPARTS .... " 59
ENCEINTE DES FANILS AND THE TOUR GABRIEL .... " 62

Printed in Italy by *Centro Stampa Editoriale Bonechi.*

Translated by *Erika Pauli, Studio Comunicare, Florence*

Distribution: OVET, 13, rue des Nanettes - 75011 Paris
Tel. (1) 43 38 57 50

ISBN 88-476-0493-1

Panorama from the southwest.

PREFACE

Mont-Saint-Michel is a marvelous image of medieval man and his society left to us by our medieval forebears. The rock looms up over a desert of sand and water. The society of man is mirrored in the hierarchy upon which Western Christianity is founded: the abbey church, on the summit, affirms the spiritual supremacy, while the ramparts demonstrate the military power that encloses the center of the village.

All around, the beach is swept twice a day by the most powerful tides in Europe. The suddenness with which the flood tide arrives, the quicksands left behind in the wake of the ebb-tide, all these threats of death so ostentatiously exaggerated in the folk tales, give the site the reputation of never-ending danger.

Thus it is that humanity, which builds ever higher as it sings God's praises, rises up above the mud. The social organization, founded on the rock and reaching skywards, is set against the void. Here myth becomes concrete reality. No better place than this to celebrate the cult of St. Michael, who in Christian religion led the forces of light in the eternal struggle against the forces of darkness. When the Middle Ages left us Mont-Saint-Michel as a legacy, they passed on to us their concept of the world, in which the imaginary and the real — far from being elements that contrast with each other — fuse to perpetuate creation and affirm unity.

The immense and apparently deserted bay gives the impression of an inhospitable waste whose distant horizons can barely be distinguished. But, the legend of a vanished forest, and miracles said to have taken place here, once more provide a link with the life and history of man. There is no better place than Mont-Saint-Michel to understand this story.

The buildings and events of which they are witness, directly or indirectly, allow us to trace all the various phases of the Middle Ages. Other Romanesque monasteries elsewhere may be better preserved, other Gothic buildings may be more daring and graceful, the city walls more structural or the old towns more authentic, but nowhere else can that continuity be found, with complete and prestigious examples of both religious, military and civil architecture, which is capable of revealing all the mysteries of the medieval period.

A marvelous microcosm, Mont-Saint-Michel and its bay are unique and their universal importance was acknowledged by UNESCO when this organization set it at

the head of its list of French sites that were declared the patrimony of the world, both from the point of view of nature and of culture.
This place is so famous that it attracts tourists from all parts of the world. The ancient abbey, at the top of the rock, is visited every year by about 650,000 tourists, half of whom are foreigners. The total number of tourists who come to the town each year is two or three times as large.
Statistics cite 1,500,000 — 1,800,000 visitors a year. Many, in fact, discouraged by the number of steps and by the summer throngs of people, often renounce climbing up to the monument which is the origin and at the same time the scope for which Mont-Saint-Michel came into being. Despite this — perhaps because the only access to the monastery is at the end of a long climb that winds through the entire town to continue at the base of the fortifications, perhaps because the view over the expanse of sand and sea is unequalled from the terrace to the west — which is actually the square in front of the abbey church — or perhaps because here all feats of architecture which make the monuments of Mont-Saint-Michel unique are so forcefully expressed — only a visit to the abbey makes even a brief visit to Mont-Saint-Michel meaningful.
Between the 10th and the 15th centuries one style succeeded another on the top of this small rock. The monks began to build at the end of those dark centuries of the early Middle Ages and continued throughout the years up to the conclusive phase of flamboyant Gothic, immediately after the Hundred Years War. A collection of precious examples for medieval art historians, the abbey is also — and perhaps above all — a demonstration of the skill of the various architects who, in their works, provided a perfect image of the life of those for whom it was built. Each moment of monastic life, each different mood finds a corresponding space, allowing each single activity to be lived in the best of ways.
Thanks to the constant presence of

Bird's-eye view of the abbey and a religious ceremony in the church.

the monastic life, obviously idealized so as to furnish the architect with a more clearly defined program, the juxtaposition of all the styles the Middle Ages produced resulted in an organic monument that was imbued with a basic harmony. At the same time the ensemble of different buildings gives an impression of great unity and abundance.
With the French Revolution the ancient abbey became the property of the state, was classified as a monument of historical interest in 1874 and is now entrusted for its preservation and care to the Ministry of Culture. Restoration carried out in the 19th century made it possible to salvage Mont-Saint-Michel and was also in part responsible for its present aspect. The bell tower and the spire, for example, — subject throughout the centuries to the actions of wind and weather — were entirely rebuilt the last time in 1897, in the styles typical of the 19th century — neo-Romanesque for the bell tower and neo-Gothic for the spire. The gilded statue of Saint Michael, also recently restored, acts as a lightning rod and protects the ensemble of buildings on the rock from further possible harm. The Mont-Saint-Michel we now all know, slender and pointed, is destined to last, even if it is a relatively recent creation.

Current restoration, which unceasingly continues, is now, with the celebration of the monastic Millennium, flanked by a desire for a spiritual rebirth. In 1969 a Benedictine community, at present consisting of seven monks, settled into the old quarters of the abbey. A mass which all worshippers may attend is celebrated daily in the abbey church which has thus in part rediscovered its original scope, lost back in 1790.
The life of the town, which is fully aware of its role as a tourist attraction, has been little changed by the return of the monks. The inhabitants of Mont-Saint-Michel have always depended for their livelihood on outsiders. The pilgrims of the Middle Ages and the 'Ancien Regime' were replaced in the 19th century by the families of the prisoners kept in the abbey which was used as a penitentiary for about 70 years. With the Belle Epoque und the arrival of tourism, the number of visitors has constantly increased. But if one wants to recapture the true atmosphere of Mont-Saint-Michel without the hordes of tourists, the best time is in winter. The rock is more beautiful than ever in the constantly changing light and the silence is broken by the cry of the thousands of sea birds which take refuge in the bay.

The Châtelet on the left and the Merveille on the right.

The buttresses of the Merveille in the north gardens.

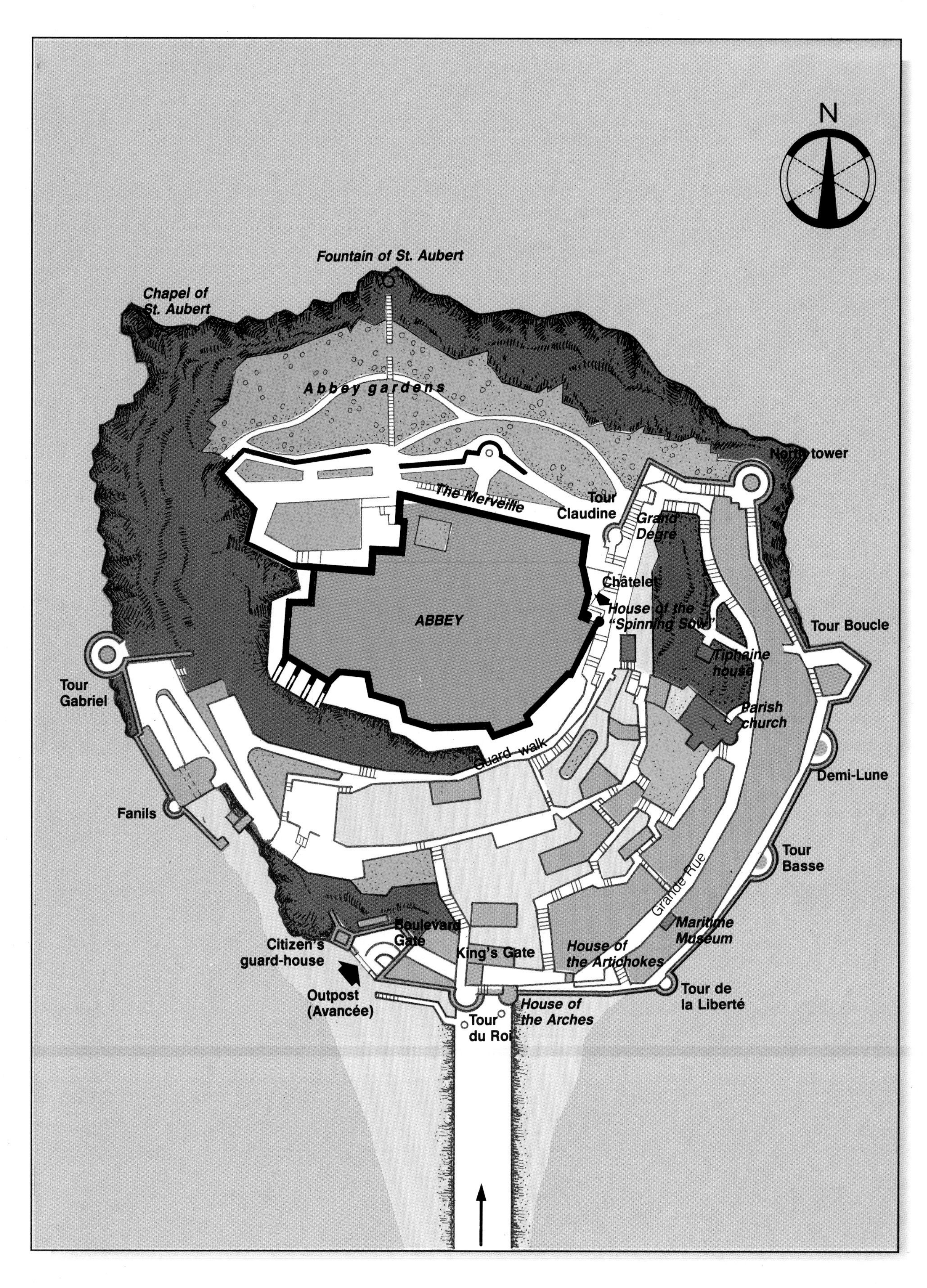
N
Fountain of St. Aubert
Chapel of St. Aubert
Abbey gardens
North tower
The Merveille
Tour Claudine
Grand Degré
Châtelet
House of the "Spinning Sow"
ABBEY
Tour Boucle
Tiphaine house
Tour Gabriel
Parish church
Guard walk
Demi-Lune
Fanils
Tour Basse
Grande Rue
Maritime Museum
Boulevard Gate
Citizen's guard-house
King's Gate
House of the Artichokes
Outpost (Avancée)
Tour de la Liberté
House of the Arches
Tour du Roi

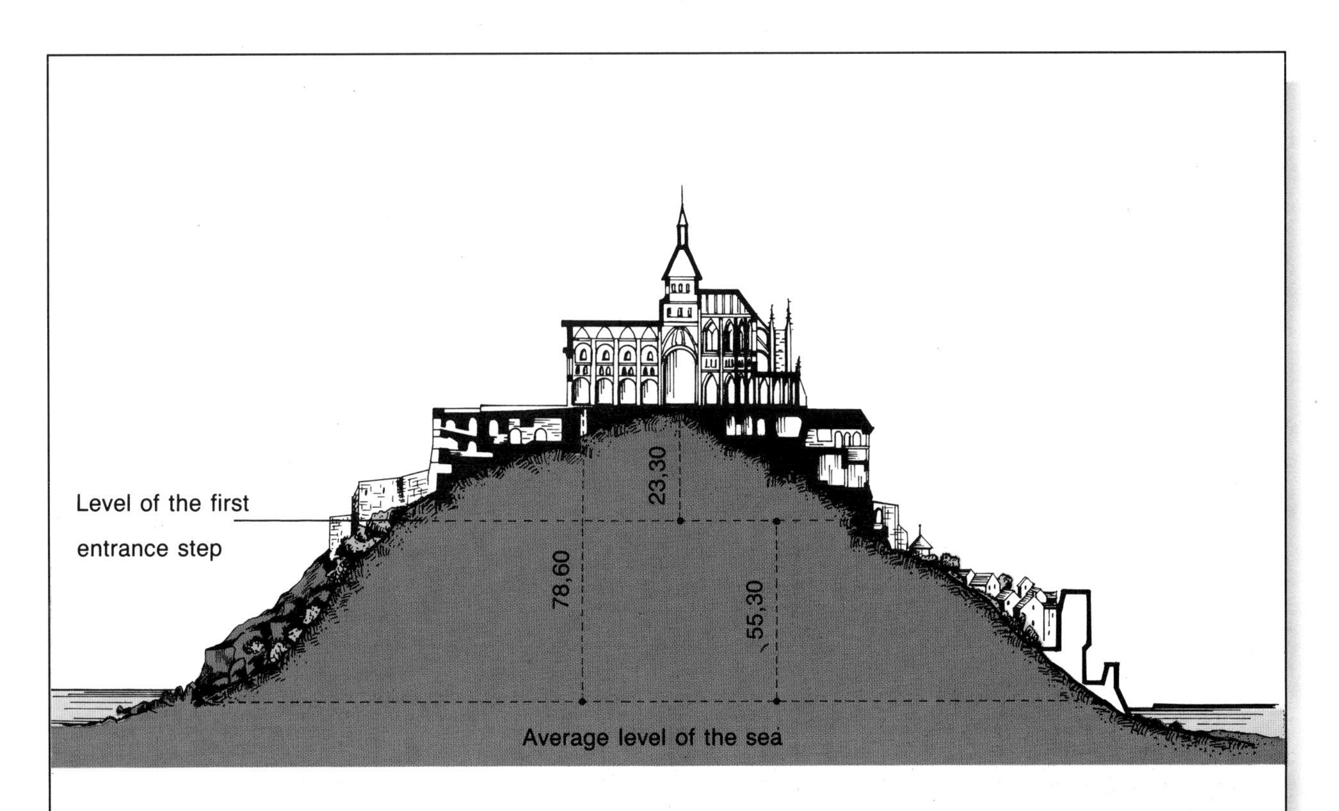

West-east cross-section of Mont-Saint-Michel.

North-south cross-section of Mont-Saint-Michel.

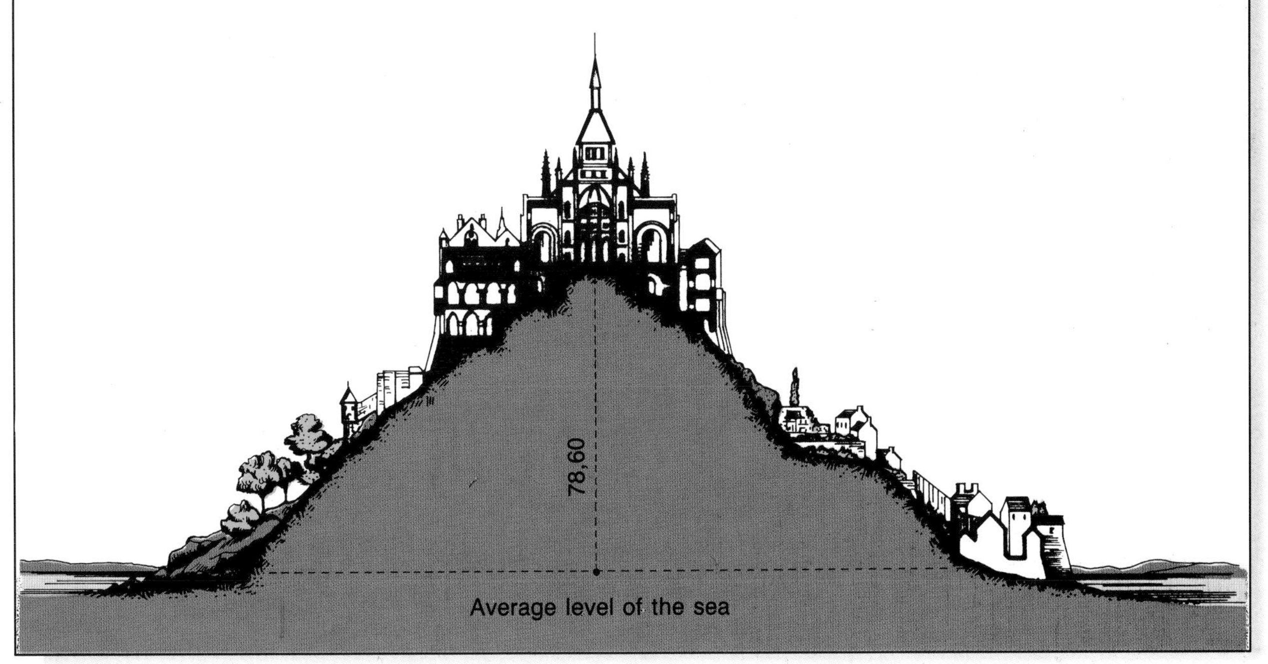

THE BAY

For a long time thought of as the jewel-case of Mont-Saint-Michel and therefore seen only as an adjunct to the whole, with the advent of ecology the bay of Mont-Saint-Michel has become the object of scientific studies and is important in its own right. It is indeed an exceptional site, the theater of surprising natural phenomena.

THE TIDES

First of all, the range of the tides. True, the difference between high tide and low tide almost always varies from a few centimeters to several meters, but in no other place in the world — except for the bay of Fundy in Canada — do the tides vary as much as here where the difference between high tide and low tide can be as much as fifteen meters.
The result of the pull of gravity exerted by the moon and to a lesser extent by the sun on the mass of water contained in the oceans, the tides rise and fall twice in every lunar day of 24 hours and 50 minutes. When the sun, the moon, and the earth are aligned, or about to be, an astronomic phenomenon known as syzygy takes place. The attraction of the two celestial bodies, together, provokes extremely strong tides, known also as spring tides. This phenomenon is particularly evident during the spring and autumn equinox, but also — and more spectacularly so — at the times of the new and full moon. High tide surrounds

Mont-Saint-Michel, the isle of Tombelaine and the bay at high tide.

Mont-Saint-Michel about seven solar hours, eight legal hours in winter and nine in summer.
On the other hand when the sun and the moon are at right angles to the earth, the pull of gravity of these two celestial bodies is in contrast. That of the moon is stronger, but in this case the range of the tides is much smaller. This is what is called a neap-tide and even at high tide the sea stops short of Mont-Saint-Michel.
The exceptional range of the tides in the bay of Mont-Saint-Michel is due to its geographical position. The movement of the tide, flowing in from the Atlantic, strikes the Cotentin almost as if it were a barrier, and the tidal waters break on the coast before entering the bay which is a cul-de-sac. In this practically flat expanse, it is obvious that a range of fifteen meters turns into an enormous distance. In periods of the so-called spring tide, the low tide withdraws as far as 18 kilometers from Mont-Saint-Michel. The flood tide of the ocean, which once rose into the Couesnon, could be seen as far as Antrain, more than 20 kilometers inland. The tides therefore went inland as much as 40 kilometers, a distance covered by the ocean in little more than six hours. Not perhaps with the speed of a galopping horse, as told in the tales, but even so still quite impressive. The speed with which the tide advances is the greatest danger in the bay where mishaps occasionally occur. A walk along the beach conceals unexpected dangers for anyone who neglects to find out beforehand just when the high tide will come in and how high it will go, and for anyone who does not make sure he is back at the rock an hour and a half before high tide. It is practically impossible for a man alone to escape from the currents and whirlpools which characterize the tides.
This real danger is flanked by that of the quicksands, consciously exaggerated by legend. The deviations of the coastal rivers into the bay have left behind in their old beds waterholes full of sand in suspension, covered by a fragile dry crust, that can easily give way under the weight of a man. Actually the quicksands are much rarer than tradition would lead one to believe. Nor should they be confused with the layers of mud, slimy deposits of sand and fine clay, which constitute one of the sedimentation levels of the bay.

High tide west of the causeway.

SILTING

In the bay of Mont-Saint-Michel the phenomenon of sedimentary deposits is such as to justify the hypothesis that a progressive silting up could before too long jeopardize the maritime character of the area. At first sight, it would seem to be a natural movement, common to all the bays in the world. The flood tide is stronger than the ebb tide and this means that more alluvial soil is brought in than out. This alluvial soil left by the ocean fills in the anfractuosity of the coasts, gulfs and bays. Around Mont-Saint-Michel the quantity of marine deposits is estimated to be around 300,000 cubic meters a year.
The lighter particles are deposited near the shore, where they form a muddy sand (called 'tangue') which consists of a mixture of very fine particles of clay, brought down by the coastal rivers, and tiny fragments of marine shells. Once, this grey sludge was used to fertilize the surrounding lands.
When deposits brought in by the sea have raised the level of the land enough to set it out of the reach of tide, plants which are able to tolerate high percentages of salt gradually begin to take hold, first of all saltwort and sea-fennel. A zone is thus formed which the inhabitants of Mont-Saint-Michel call 'herbu' (literally grassy) better known in the rest of the world as salt marsh. These plants in turn help to retain the marine sediments, accellerating the process of silting.
For centuries, the bay of Mont-Saint-Michel has succeeded in avoiding this phenomenon. The existence of numerous streams along the coast — the Couesnon, the river of Ardevon, the Guintre, the river of Huisnes, the Sélune and the Sée, — together with the range of the tides explain why. Each of these rivers, no more than a rivulet in the period of neap-tides, became a rushing stream when the tides penetrated inland and flooded vast areas of swampland. At low tide the considerable masses of water thus formed returned to the sea, forming impressive waterfalls which swept the bay clear of all the deposits left by the high tide. The deviation of these rivers in the direction of the bay sometimes brought them up to the shore where they could seriously damage crops. Tradition narrates that various coastal

towns disappeared completely during the Middle Ages. The first attempts to transform the fertile muddy sand of the bay into arable land date to the 11th century. At the beginning of the 13th century, the bishop of Dol ordered various dams to be constructed which would protect the black swamps (marais noirs) from the sea and the rivers. Mont-Dol, which once rose upon the sand like Tombelaine and Mont-Saint-Michel, thus found itself surrounded by land. Up until the end of the 19th century, however, the area between the rivers Sée and Couesnon continued to be subject to strong currents which made it impossible to construct polders and reclaim the land.

The concession granted Mosselman and Donon in 1856 was a turning point in the history of the bay. Thanks to the new techniques imported from Holland, the Couesnon was canalized up to less than two kilometers from Mont-Saint-Michel. The rivers Sée and Sélune were deviated northwards thanks to a submarine dam, set on the rocky point of Roche-Torin, and the numerous streams which formerly flowed into the Couesnon and the Sélune were also directed here. Protected from the deviation of the rivers, the bottom of the bay thus became a vast container for sediments.

The building of a causeway in 1877, despite the opposition of the State Council of Fine Arts, was still another stage in the polderization, which was concluded in 1936. The Association of the Friends of Mont-Saint-Michel had been fighting for 15 years to keep the Mont an island and while they were unsuccessful in halting work on the causeway, they succeeded in getting the public forces to limit the arable lands to no closer than one and a half kilometers from the rock.

The creation of new polders was thus stopped once and for all. But this did not do away with the modifications that had been made to the rivers in the bay, the principal reasons for the silting up. Indeed the grasslands still kept on expanding towards Mont-Saint-Michel.

Scientific studies were begun in 1974 in an attempt to find some way that would allow Mont-Saint-Michel to preserve its maritime character without infringing on the rights acquired by the farmers of the polders. Sponsored by the Central Hydraulic Laboratory, these studies have demonstrated that it was possible to lower the level of the sands by reintegrating the water holes, which, up to the 19th century, had kept the bay naturally clean.

The technicians outlined a plan in three phases: first, the basin of the Couesnon had to be regulated so that the tide waters could flow into the lower course of the river and constitute a basin which would rapidly empty with the ebb tide. The second phase provided for the creation of a series of artificial tide reservoirs, which would function on the same principle, to the east of the causeway. The third phase consisted in the dismantling of the dam of Roche-Torin, so that the Sée and Sé-

Many species of migratory fowl have always wintered in the bay around Mont-Saint-Michel.

An alophyte, one of the few types of plants that grow in the salt-laden earth of the bay.

The unique breed of sheep which pasture in the salt marshes.

lune rivers could deepen the eastern part of the bay.
Work began in 1983 on the third phase, which was the simplest from the technical and juridical point of view. The regulation of the Couesnon basin is to be undertaken fairly soon, in the hopes that the pessimistic forecast of the Central Laboratory of Hydraulics that the point of no return will be reached in 1991 may finally be proved wrong.

THE FAUNA

The dredging of the zone will considerably reduce the pasture areas and as a result the number of sheep which graze on the salt marsh. This unique race was bred in the Avranchin in the 19th century and can be easily identified by the shape of the head and the black legs. Feeding on these grasslands, their savory meat is known and appreciated in zones far from Mont-Saint-Michel.
The wildlife, which consists mostly of birds, is much more heterogenous.
The bay constitutes an ideal refuge for migratory birds, especially the anatides, which spend the winter here. There are also numerous ducks, prevalently mallards but also rarer species such as the sheldrakes of Belon, which nest on the polder dams or the reefs of Tombelaine. With a bit of good luck, observing the shore it may also be possible to glimpse a barnacle-goose or some other kind of wild bird.
While these migratory birds winter here, there are others for whom the bay of Mont-Saint-Michel is but a way station: herons, pink flamingos, more rarely a wild swan.
By far the most numerous, however, are those birds whose natural habitat is the bay. All kinds of gulls, sea swallows, and even an occasional large cormorant.
The bay is also populated by other animals but they are more difficult to see — the fishes, above all grey mullet, flounders, bass. In the 19th century, fishing was one of the principal activities of the inhabitants of Mont-Saint-Michel while the women gathered the small clams which lived in dense banks in the sand.

THE CITY

Enclosed within bastions and nestled at the foot of the monastery, the village of Mont-Saint-Michel is a city in the eyes of those who live there. It was born from the abbey and still lives in its shade, for what makes the town unique and attracts tourists to Mont-Saint-Michel is the abbey.
The origins of the town can presumably be linked to the pilgrims who early began to arrive, drawn by the fame of the sanctuary.
The first innkeepers provided hospitality, tavern keepers offered meals, merchants holy images, figures of St. Michael or something that had to do with his cult, sold them the first souvenirs. They were the ancestors, in other words, of the hotel keepers, restaurant owners and souvenir venders of today.
The atmosphere in the town is not after all so different from what it was centuries ago.
The village seems to have been organized so as to cluster around the entrance to the abbey, in the best position to profit from the passage of the pilgrims, and later of the tourists. When the Bretons fired the village in 1204, the flames spread to the abbey and gutted Mont-Saint-Michel.
The buildings that were destroyed were situated on the north flank of the rock, on the site of the Merveille. The entrance to the monastery at the time must therefore have been on the northwest, and the first urban settlement must then have faced out to sea in the direction of Tombelaine. The present layout of the houses and shops would therefore date back only to the first half of the 13th century. The entire city winds along the only road which climbs up the southeast side of the mountain, from the beach up to the monastery. Behind this route which the tourist follows, is a variety of lanes and alleys, often breaking into steep flights of steps, which provide shortcuts to the abbey. One of these, the alley known as 'le chemin des monteux' passes along the top of the western fortifications, departing from the King's Gate. Other lanes cross the main street; the oddest is the one that passes under the choir of the parish church and runs along the edge of the small cemetery.
A parish under the 'Ancien Regime' and subjected to the abbey, the city became an autonomous commune under the Revolution and such it has remained.
The creation of the polders has allowed the town to expand beyond the circle of the rock, thanks to the annexation of part of the lands won from the sea in the 19th century. In a certain sense, Mont-Saint-Michel is then a rural township.
About thirty people live permanently in the town, but the voting list contains more than a hundred names. Evidently the tradesmen prefer to vote where they work rather than on the continent.

The village nestles at the foot of the abbey enclosed within bastions.

THE DEFENSES

The village underwent its greatest period of development during the Hundred Years War when 119 knights established themselves in the fortress and successfully defended it against the English. This was when the first ramparts were built and particular attention was obviously paid to the defenses of the city gates. To enter, three successive fortified gates had to be passed.
The first of these, the **Outpost (Avancée),** was not added until the 16th century, to counteract the progress that had been made in the field of artillery. It is defended by the citizen's guard-house, a small granite building roofed with slate which now houses the Tourist Office. It leads into a first defensive area in which the 'michelettes', mortars abandoned by the English in the Hundred Years War, during the abortive attack of 1434, are displayed.
The second of the city gates is the **Boulevard Gate,** which takes its name from the defensive area set in front of the principal fortifications to defend them from artillery attacks. Unfortunately the site was ruined when the hôtel de la Mère Poulard was built in the 'Belle Epoque'.
The third is the **King's Gate (Porte du Roi),** surely built for Robert Jolivet, abbot of Mont-Saint-Michel before it passed to the English in 1420. It was preceded by a moat with a drawbridge, and closed by a portcullis that is still in place, although obviously very rusted and no longer in working order. Only one of the two towers which flanked the gate is still visible. The other was swallowed up by the hôtel de la Mère Poulard. Oddly enough, while two openings existed on the outer side, one for wagons and the other for pedestrians, there is only one on the inside toward the town. Above the wagon gate is an escutcheon

The outpost called Porte de l'Avancée, the fortified courtyard with the Boulevard Gate and the mortars known as "michelettes".

The King's Gate with the coats of arms of the king, the abbot, and the city.

with the coats of arms of the king, the monastery and the town. The guard walk on the ramparts continues on the upper level. It can be reached by a small flight of stairs which runs along the wall right inside the gate, and continues towards the abbey and the stairs the inhabitants of the town call Le Monteaux.

The King's Gate takes its name from the living quarters on the ground floor which were destined for whoever guarded it in the name of the King of France. Today it is the town hall of Mont-Saint-Michel.

THE OLD HOUSES

The old town of Mont-Saint-Michel consisted principally of timber-framed houses. Most of them were torn down in the Belle Epoque and replaced by more comfortable dwellings which however respected the original division into lots. Some of them still exist.
The **house of the Arches**, constructed on corbels as if it were clinging to the ramparts, is just inside and facing the King's Gate. It once housed part of the garrison. Not far off is the **house of the Artichoke** which takes its name from the floret of its dormer windows and forms a bridge across the street. The **Inn of the Unicorn** now houses a souvenir shop and a crêperie. It is the last example of the houses which once characterized Mont-Saint-Michel. Right across is the **hôtel Saint-Pierre**, which merits a few words for it is a real pastiche, built in the winter of 1986-87, respecting the all-over volume as furnished by the model of Mont-Saint-Michel realized in 1701 and of which the abbey has a copy.
The house know as the **house of Guesclin and his wife Tiphaine** is an example, albeit greatly restored, of the few old houses in stone. The **shop of the White Ram (Mouton Blanc)**, right across from the hotel of the same name, once housed the old town bakery.

Some of the most interesting old houses in the village: the House of the Arches, the House of the Artichokes, and the Tiphaine House.

COMMERCE

In a place dedicated from the very beginning to providing hospitality for strangers, the name of Mère Poulard is inscindable from the birth of tourism. After the prison was shut, Annette Poulard was the first to take in the visitors who came to see the abbey which had been opened to the public. She became famous for her exquisite courtesy and for the tasty omelette she whipped up in the wink of an eye for those who were in a hurry. The roads of Mont-Saint-Michel are densely lined with hotels, restaurants and souvenir shops. They represent the activities to which the population is traditionally dedicated although up the 1950s fishing was also important. After World War II, however, tourism predominated and no room was left for the fishermen or the 'coquetières' (clam diggers).
The overwhelming development of tourism and the charm of the past which brings throngs of visitors to Mont-Saint-Michel each year induced a businessman to open an essentially commercial 'historical museum' at the end of the 19th century. The same idea was exploited by the 'Tiphaine house' and the 'maritime museum'. The 'Archeoscope'', inaugurated in 1988, will permit this branch to be thoroughly renewed by introducing a historically exact presentation, based on the spectacular technology in use.

The inn sign of the famous Hôtel de la Mère Poulard, the model of the Mont in the Archeoscope and a view of the street.

THE PARISH CHURCH

Dedicated to St. Peter, the parish church of Mont-Saint-Michel replaced an ancient sanctuary that may even date to before the introduction of the cult of St. Michael.
Built on foundations that probably date to the 11th century, the building was enlarged and raised in the second half of the 15th century. The odd 16th-century addition is on a barrel vault built over a lane.
At the end of the 19th century, when the abbey was secularized, the church became the goal of pilgrimages. The restoration of the chapel dedicated to the Archangel which contains a *statue* of him *in silver* that was solemnly crowned in 1877, bears witness to the vitality of the cult of St. Michael in the context of renewed patriotism which came to the fore after the war of 1870. The many *ex-votos* hung on the walls are often of military origin, in homage to the patron saint of the armed forces. The *gonfalons* offered by the brotherhoods of the faithful also demonstrate the popular character of the pilgrimages.
All these objects more or less overshadow the few remaining old elements, in particular the 13th-century *baptismal fonts*, a 15th-century *statue of a Madonna and Child*, another 16th-century *statue of St. Anne* and an 18th-century *crucifix.*
Heart of parish life in Mont-Saint-Michel, the church stands next to the small town cemetery. Mère Poulard lies buried here and the inscription on her tomb reads: "Here rest Victor and Anne Poulard, faithful husband and wife and good innkeepers. May the Lord receive them as they have always received their guests."

The exterior of the parish church of St. Peter with its small cemetery. Inside the church is a silver statue of St. Michael defeating the dragon.

THE ABBEY

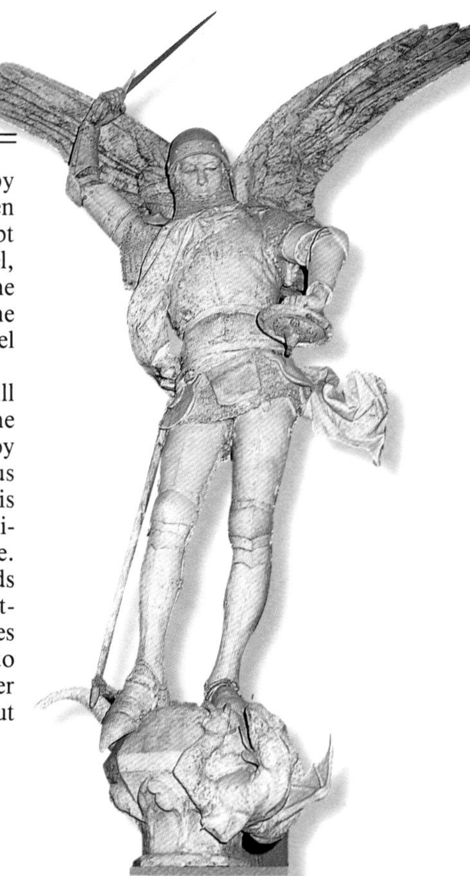

THE FOUNDATION OF THE ABBEY

A tradition that dates back to the 10th century narrates that the Archangel appeared to St. Aubert, bishop of Avranches, in a dream and asked him to build a church dedicated to St. Michael on top of the rock which up to then had been called Mount Tombe.
This legend is similar to the one relating to the construction on Monte Gargano, in the heel of the boot of Italy, of the first sanctuary in the west ever dedicated to the archangel Michael. As then, here too, the bishop of the neighboring city arrived on the spot indicated by the angel only after his third appearance. And as then, here too, the precise site was indicated by the presence of a bull that had been stolen and was hidden there. Except that in the case of Mont-Saint-Michel, St. Aubert had the church built in the form of a cave, in imitation of the natural grotto in which St. Michael had appeared in Italy.
Apparently, for reasons that are still not clear, what we have here in the region of Avranchin is the exact copy of a pilgrimage site that was famous throughout the west. For many this could be interpreted as the christianization of a pre-existing pagan temple. This hypothesis, however, is at odds with the existence on Mont-Saint-Michel of two Christian oratories probably dating to the 6th century to which reference is made in the older version of the legend. Others, without

The entrance to the abbey of Monte S. Angelo on the Gargano, original plaster cast of the statue which is at the top of the spire, by Frémiet, and what remains of the first sanctuary in the church of Notre Dame sous Terre.

any backing whatsoever, attribute the foundation of Mont-Saint-Michel to a group of Irish monks. The most plausible hypothesis on the other hand justifies the introduction of the cult of the archangel who defeated Satan to the specific political significance of Avranchin in the context of the Merovingian realm.
Whatever the case may be, the construction on the rock of the first church dedicated to St. Michael does seem to date to the 8th century. The church may have been inside a monastery which already had a series of sanctuaries. A wall in large irregular blocks of dressed stone, sometimes improperly denominated Cyclopean, was brought to light by Y. M. Froidevaux under the present Notre Dame sous Terre.
St. Aubert assigned the oratory he had built to a community of canons about whom we know practically nothing. Reference to them appears in the tales of a pilgrimage which passed through in the year 860. The community then seems to have passed under the authority of the Bretons, to whom Charles the Bald had conceded the diocese of Avranches. This was the period of the Norman invasions and the community of Mont-Saint-Michel was the only one on the coasts of France not to disappear under the assaults of the marauders.

The Carolingian church of Notre Dame sous Terre is the oldest monument on the Mont.

THE CAROLINGIAN CHURCH

It was probably at this time that the first Carolingian church known as Notre Dame sous Terre was built on the site of St. Aubert's man-made grotto.
This is the oldest existing monument on Mont-Saint-Michel. Built on the western side of the rock, it was surrounded by nothing but a few canons' houses and by a building, no longer extant, which stood on the top of the Mont. One can imagine how much light must have streamed in through the windows that were walled up in the 11th century when Notre Dame sous Terre was incorporated into the foundations of the Romanesque abbey.
No one knows why this church has two aisles. It may have been an attempt to perpetuate the memory of the original bond with Mt. Gargano, where the cave is approximately heart-shaped. Perhaps Notre Dame sous Terre was divided after its construction so that it might be vaulted in stone. Perhaps the ground plan reflects the liturgy of the canons, which we no longer know, or the fusion into a single building of two sanctuaries of a non-Benedictine monastery where more than one were allowed.
The use of brick in the construction of the arches would seem to indicate that the church was inspired by the Gallo-Roman monuments which probably still existed in the 10th century — not at Mont-Saint-Michel itself but in the region. The static juxtaposition of volumes in the two aisles and their apses closely recalls

ancient Roman architecture.
Incorporated in the 11th century into the supports of the Romanesque nave, obstructed apparently in the 12th century by a superfluous pillar which disfigured the entire north aisle, the church was partially walled up in the 18th century when the Maurist monks built the present facade of the abbey church. It is thanks to the work undertaken by the architect of historical monuments, Y. M. Froidevaux, who reinforced the vault with precompressed reinforced concrete that Notre Dame sous Terre has once more regained its original proportions.

THE BENEDICTINE ABBEY

The community of canons which had lived in Mont-Saint-Michel ever since the beginning of the 8th century was expelled by the duke of Normandy, Richard I. He accused the canons of leading too lax and secular a life but the real reason was probably that he was preoccupied by the ties that still existed between the canons and the Bretons, particularly in view of the uneasy frontier. To celebrate the cult of St. Michael the duke called in the Benedictine monks with whom he had recently come to terms with a view to constructing Normandy politically, intellectually and spiritually. In 966 twelve monks under the guidance of Abbot Maynard arrived from Saint-Wandrille to turn the Mont into a great Benedictine abbey. From then on Mont-Saint-Michel was to live according to the rhythm imparted by the rules of St. Benedict. The medieval monks lived to sing the praises of the Lord and with their liturgy to anticipate the Celestial Jerusalem. They thought of themselves as the militia called to fight for the Lord on earth, under the authority of the abbot. Like the knights, who fought for the duke guided by their baron. Like St. Michael, in heaven, against Satan.
To perform their duty, the monks sang eight offices a day. The rest of the time was divided between work and the material obligations of daily life. The Benedictine rule aimed at a certain balance, in sharp contrast with the rules which generally regulated the lives of other monks.
Great importance was also set on hospitality, although of course the Benedictine monasteries were not transformed into hospitaller monasteries. Moreover in Mont-Saint-Michel the importance attributed to pilgrimages may be one reason for the limited number of monks, for there were never in fact more than sixty.

The western facade of the Romanesque convent buildings.

Illuminated letter P, mid-10th century. Municipal Library of Avranches, MS 101.

PLAN OF THE TOP FLOOR OF THE ABBEY

(abbey church).

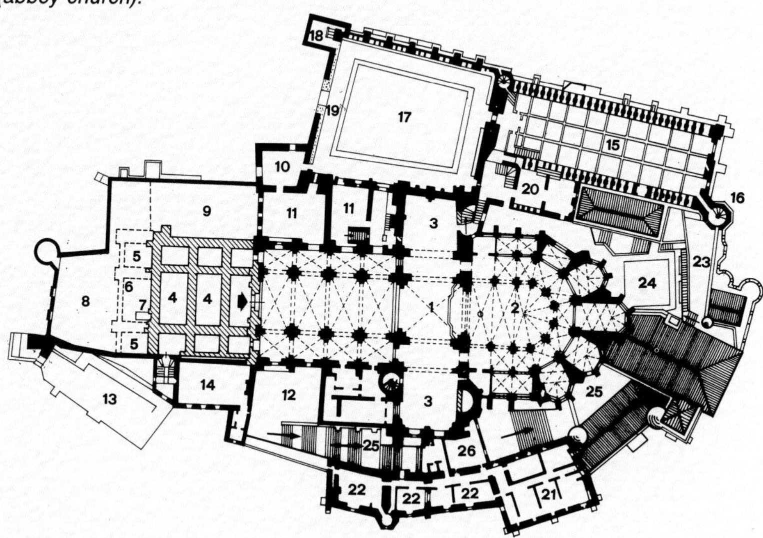

1 The upper church
2 The choir
3 The north transept and the south transept
4 The first bays of the Romanesque nave
5 The towers in front of the Romanesque portal
6 Porch between the two towers
7 Tomb of R. de Torigny and of D.M. de Furmendeio (?)
8 The old outer sanctuary
9 Chapter Hall; old dormitory
10 Old abbey buildings
11 The present sacristy
12 Platform of Saut-Gautier
13 Ruins of the hostelry
14 Infirmary
15 Refectory (The Merveille)
16 Tour des Corbins (The Merveille)
17 Cloister (The Merveille)
18 Archives
19 Entrance to the chapter hall
20 Kitchens
21 Abbot's lodging
22 Abbey lodgings
23 Courtyard of the Merveille
24 Apse terrace
25 Courtyard and staircase to Saut-Gautier
26 The present kitchens

PLAN OF THE INTERMEDIATE FLOOR OF THE ABBEY

(crypt, Salle des Hôtes and Salle des Chevaliers).

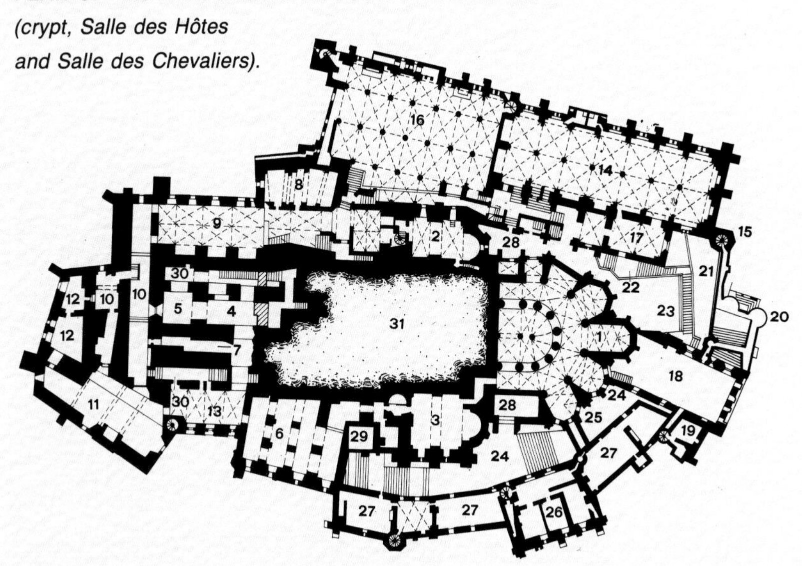

1 Crypte des Gros Piliers
2 Chapel under the north transept
3 Chapel under the south transept
4 Substructures of the Romanesque nave
5 The monks' cemetery
6 Romanesque substructures
7 Ancient cistern
8 Old abbey buildings - Refectory
9 Ancient cloister or Promenoir
10 Communication passageways with the hostelry
11 Hostelry
12 Lodgings annexed to the hostelry
13 Chapel of St. Stephen
14 Salle des hôtes (The Merveille)
15 Tour des Corbins (The Merveille)
16 Salle des Chevaliers (The Merveille)
17 Chapel of St. Magdalene
18 Room of the Officers or the Government (Belle-Chaise)
19 Tour Perrine
20 Crenellation of the Châtelet
21 Courtyard of the Merveille
22 Staircase
23 Apse terrace
24 Courtyard of the church
25 Fortified bridge
26 Abbot's lodgings
27 Lodgings of the Abbey
28 Cisterns
29 Cistern
30 Staircase
31 The rock

PLAN OF THE LOWER FLOOR OF THE ABBEY

(cellar and almonry).

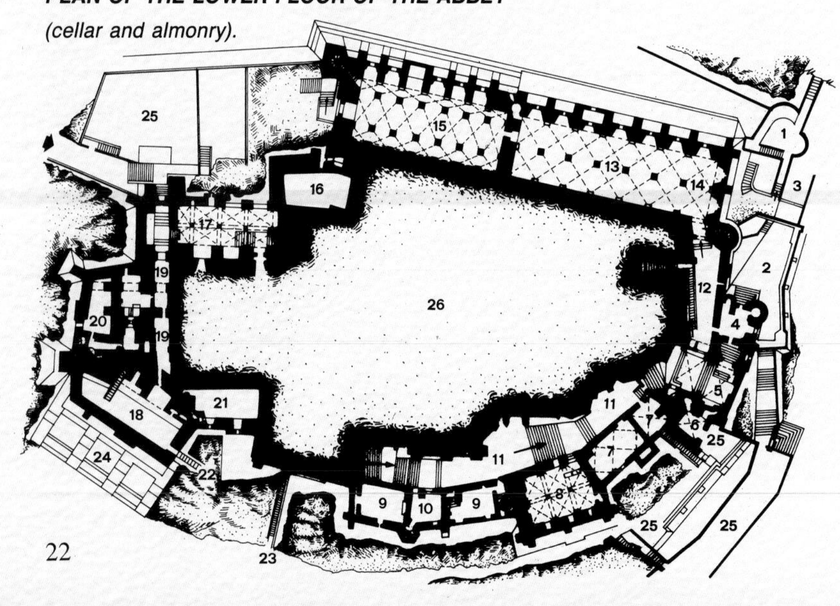

1 Tour Claudine
2 The barbican
3 The staircase called the Grand Degré
4 The Châtelet
5 The Guard Room
6 Tour Perrine
7 Lodgings of the steward and bailiff of the Abbey
8 Abbot's lodging
9 Abbey lodgings
10 Chapel of St. Catherine
11 The courtyard and stairs to the upper church
12 Courtyard of the Merveille
13 Room of the Almonry (The Merveille)
14 Ruins of an oven (The Merveille)
15 Cellar or storeroom (The Merveille)
16 Old abbey structures - The kitchens
17 The Crypte de l'Aquilon
18 Substructures of the hostelry
19 Passageways communicating with the hostelry
20 The prisons
21 Basement of St. Stephen's Chapel
22 Ruins of the old slide-lift
23 The modern slide-lift
24 Supporting walls
25 Gardens, terraces and guard walks
26 The rock

THE ABBEY CHURCH

The construction of the abbey church of Mont-Saint-Michel is one of the most daring examples of medieval architecture.
A new style of architecture developed throughout western Europe at the beginning of the 11th century. It was essentially monastic, characterized by large churches, with stone vaults and a ground plan in the form of a cross. On Mont-Saint-Michel, the sanctuary of the archangel Michael was still the small Carolingian church of Notre Dame sous Terre, when the increasing importance of the pilgrimages and the prestige of the Benedictine abbey necessitated a church built, as in the most important abbeys, in the new style of the period, now called Romanesque.
In 1022 the duke of Normandy Richard II provided the funds for the reconstruction of the church. But the main problem was of a purely technical nature — nowhere on the cone of granite of Mont-Saint-Michel was there a level surface large enough for the construction of a building seventy meters long. The builders therefore decided to erect the center of the church on the top of the rock and surround it with a series of crypts which would serve as foundations for the choir and the arms of the transept, bringing them up to the level of the nave.
On the west, the nave was set almost entirely on the Carolingian church, which was transformed into a supporting crypt. Only the crossing and the three bays of the nave were thus built directly on the rock, while the greater part of the large abbey church which rises above Mont-Saint-Michel was built on various levels.
Unfortunately, in the course of the centuries the sanctuary suffered various mutilations, including the destruction of the Romanesque choir in the 15th century and the reduction of the nave by about half in the 18th century.

The portal of the church which overlooks the so-called "Saut-Gautier" terrace.

THE NAVE

Of the seven bays the nave of the abbey church of Mont-Saint-Michel originally had, four — of which three have disappeared — rested on the Carolingian church of Notre Dame sous Terre. Despite this, the Romanesque architect conceived of an elevation on three levels, comparable to that of the largest churches then being built in Normandy.

Norman 11th-century naves are in fact characterized by the superposition of large arches, of galleries or false galleries, and tall windows. This interior elevation, which heralds that of the Gothic cathedrals a century later, was made possible by the wooden ceiling which not only weighed less than a stone vault, but which also exerted less thrust on the walls. In this aspect the church clearly betrays its Norman identity.

Observing the nave, one becomes aware of the differences between the two sides. The whole north side, which collapsed barely twenty years after it was finished, had to be entirely rebuilt at the beginning of the 12th century. An analysis of the differences to be found in the two walls reveals the differences in architectural concept.

In the 11th century the technique was still crude. The arches of the large arcades, as is also the case for the transverse arches of the aisles, were built in rubble masonry between two facings of dressed stone. The masonry has gradually been compressed under the weight and the cross arches of the aisles have taken on the form of basket-handle arches.

When the north side had to be rebuilt the technique had improved considerably. The arches are built entirely of hewn stone which cannot be compressed like the mortar of the 11th century. The stones are also slightly tapered, thus reducing the lateral thrust and making the whole building more stable. But despite this undeniable progress in building techniques, the 12th-century architect lacked the

The Romanesque nave of the abbey church built over the church of Notre Dame sous Terre.

General view of the abbey church: the Romanesque nave and the flamboyant Gothic choir. ▶

The south wall of the nave (11th cent.).

The north wall (12th cent.).

The two arms of the transept and the two crypts underneath: Our Lady of the Thirty Tapers on the north, Saint Martin on the south. ▶

creative daring of his predecessors. The north wall of the nave is too massive, the galleries have openings that are too small. This whole side furnishes an effect of mass.
By comparison, the south side, even though it is earlier, appears lighter, the half columns that rise to the wooden vault are set against piers which, at the top of the wall, join and form large arches which divert the thrust. The weight of the upper part is thus carried directly to the piers and the thrust is concentrated on the same principle that, a hundred years later, was to be used in Gothic architecture.
In addition these arches stress the unity of each bay, thus helping to create the rhythm of the nave. The openings of the galleries are separated only by a small pier flanked by two half columns so that the overall effect is that of an opening rather than that of a wall.
As generally was the case in 11th-century Normandy, an extremely simple decoration accompanied the highly creative architecture. Most of the sculpture was replaced after a fire which destroyed the nave in 1834. The few original capitals that managed to survive are in poor condition and seem heavy, as if they had been hard to carve in the granite.
Despite these mutilations and reconstructions, the nave of the abbey church of Mont-Saint-Michel continues to be living proof of the daring of those who planned it. Even though the interior as a spatial entity is no longer what the 11th-century architect had envisioned, even though the brilliant colored setting of the Benedictine liturgy no longer exists, what remains is still enough to make us realize how extraordinary the inventive daring and the tenacity of the medieval builders was.

THE TRANSEPT

A few years earlier than the nave, the transept of the abbey church was built between 1030 and 1048. The crossing, together with the neighboring three bays of the nave, is the only part of the building that rests directly on the rock. Crushed under the weight of an overly massive bell tower, the crossing was completely rebuilt at the end of the 19th century, from the ground up to the tip of the spire.
On the north and the south, the two arms were raised over crypts. On the south, the one dedicated to St. Martin is still intact. Only that it has lost

the painting which once lined the walls, so that now the traces of the wooden scaffolding used in its construction can be clearly seen in the barrel vault. On the north, the crypt of *Our Lady of the Thirty Tapers* was slightly modified in the course of the 13th century. It consists of a cross vault which preserves important vestiges of murals: two sections are painted with a pattern of faux stonework, very popular in the Romanesque period, and decorated with a frieze of foliage.
Even though the principal role of the crypts was that of supporting the arms of the transept, the space inside is that of a real chapel. The spatial unity imparted by the vaults and the transversals in the ceiling turns the crypts into self-sufficient works of architecture, independent of the monument they support. The small apses which open off to the east under the large buttressing arches give them a meaning, a spiritual value. They demonstrate that for 11th-century man the foundation of a church could not be anything but another place of worship.
On the *floor above*, the two arms of the transept are covered with barrel vaults. Like those in the crypts, they represent one of the first attempts made in the Middle Ages to cover such large areas with stone. In the 13th century, when room was needed to the north of the church for the complex of the Merveille, the gable end of the north arm was rebuilt with a set of large Gothic windows.
The importance of the transept in the spiritual life is emphasized not only by the stone vaulting, generally reserved to the parts of the church in which the offices were celebrated, but also by the quality of the decoration. The arches of the windows spring from small twin columns and the use of imported stone for the capitals, in Corinthian style, led to an exceedingly fine sculpture, the likes of which are found nowhere else in the Romanesque monastery.

The crypt of Our Lady of the Thirty Tapers which supports the north arm of the transept.

The facade of the 11th-century convent buildings seen from the north gardens.

THE ROMANESQUE BUILDINGS OF THE CONVENT

The conical shape of the rock which had led the builders of the church to construct a ring of crypts, also prevented them from giving a traditional plan to the convent buildings. In all other monasteries, these buildings are organized around a cloister set in the corner between the nave and the transept. For Mont-Saint-Michel the traditional ground plan had to be inverted, and the abbey had to be built with rooms set one on top of the other instead of next to each other.
The first convent buildings went up together with the nave, set against the north wall, in the second half of the 11th century. The largest of these was spread out over three levels and included the most important rooms in the monastery: on the upper floor the dormitory communicated directly with the abbey church, so that the monks could attend services at night without having to go outside. The intermediate floor contained a large room now known as the *promenoir*, which was probably a general duty room. On the ground floor, the *Crypte de l'Aquilon*, was the almonry in which the poor assisted by the abbey were received.
Only half of the second building is still standing. The wing destroyed in the 18th century was also planned on three levels: the ground floor was the lateral extension of the Aquilon crypt, with a square ground plan; on the upper level another room that may have been a kitchen opened onto the *promenoir*. Nothing is known of the rooms that were on the top level of this wing. What is left of this building has only two floors: a small room traditionally know as the old infirmary still communicates with the dormitory. The space underneath must have contained the latrines.
In the 11th century the entrance to the abbey was on the north side while the galleries and access stairs to the monastery buildings as well as the ground floor of the building to the north were the equivalent of the first courtyard of the other abbeys, to which lay persons also had free access. The monastery enclosure, the part that is reserved for the monks, housing the different activities, was on the upper floors of the north building, directly over the almonry.

THE DORMITORY

The monks' dormitory was originally a spacious room, as long as the nave, both of which were shortened in 1776. Nothing but a small part, that has often been tampered with, still remains. The walls have been rebuilt so often throughout the years that a precise reconstruction is impossible.
The dormitory is covered with a plastered wooden ceiling as it originally was. It now houses a permanent exhibition open to the public on the historical development of Mont-Saint-Michel.

THE PROMENOIR

The promenoir which lies under the dormitory is the only large room of the convent buildings which dates back to the 11th century. The name, which makes one think it was used rather like a cloister, is relatively recent. The room is divided into two aisles by a cluster of columns. It was initally covered with a wooden ceiling and cross rib vaulting in the 12th century. A door leads to a guard walk which ran along inside the wall and connected the various rooms. Since diverse parts of the Romanesque buildings no longer exist it is no longer practicable.

THE CRYPTE DE L'AQUILON

With its heavy cross vaulting, this Romanesque almonry is at present illuminated by two large openings in the north wall which originally must have led, at the back of the room, to a structure that no longer exists.
The ease of access to this room situated right next to the entrance was why a small watchpost was set up in the northwest corner, integrating the guard walk which began at the promenoir.

The superposed rooms of the dormitory, the promenoir and the Crypte de l'Aquilon.

Watchpost in the Romanesque almonry.

The north-south staircase which supported the Romanesque facade of the abbey church.

ENTRANCES TO THE ROMANESQUE ABBEY

From the 11th to the 13th century the entrance to the monastery was situated in the northwest corner of the convent buildings. A sort of large courtyard opened here, which has now been altered and partitioned and which provided access both to the almonry and, via flights of stairs, to the abbey church.
The main staircase, oriented north-south, crosses the entire abbey passing under the Romanesque facade of the church, for which it once served as support. The west side led to the ecclesiastical court, set above the entrance courtyard. In the 11th century this was the only room used for secular purposes and the management of the monastery holdings took place here. On the upper floor an elbow bend was planned which, once built, would have provided access, under the offices, to the entrance of the abbey church. The majestic north-south staircase remained unfinished and therefore never actually provided the solemn access to the sanctuary that had been intended.
It is difficult nowadays to imagine what life in these buildings must have been like in the 11th century. Modifications. collapse, fires have left deep marks on their history. These Romanesque rooms now seem melancholy and cold but we must clothe them mentally with the frescoes that once covered the walls and envision the spaces animated by monastic life. Moreover not even the 11th-century abbey was ever finished. As long as the monks lived there it was always a construction yard. Various buildings were added on the north early in the 12th century. They were however destroyed in the fire of 1204 and made way for the complex of the *Merveille* at the beginning of the 13th century. The collapse of the north wall of the nave, in which the ceilings were also destroyed, followed by a fire in 1138, forced the monks to endlessly continue their rebuilding. But the most important modifications ever effectuated on the Romanesque abbey were carried out under Robert de Torigny, a famous abbot in the second half of the 12th century.

ROBERT DE TORIGNY'S APARTMENTS

Around the second half of the 12th century the most famous abbot of Mont-Saint-Michel, Robert de Torigny, had his personal lodgings built at the western extremity of the monastery. These two small modest rooms, access to which is through the bishop's office of the 11th century, were built in a technique which was really no longer fashionable in the 12th century, for they are covered with heavy pointed barrel vaults which exert an enormous thrust on the walls. In addition, the weight of the two towers on the facade of the nearby bishop's office caused rather serious damage to the masonry.

These two rooms bear witness to the fact that an important modification had taken place in the communal life of the monks. Up to the time when they were built, the abbot seems to have respected the rule of St. Benedict which required him to sleep in the dormitory with the other monks. By building his lodgings near the office of the ecclesiastic court, Robert de Torigny demonstrated how much space the administration of the abbey's temporal power occupied in his life. This is the beginning of that movement which was to lead first to the construction of the gigantic monastic lodgings which crown the abbey on the south, and then to the institution of the benefice "in commendam" in the 16th century.

THE PORTER'S LODGINGS AND THE DUNGEONS

The two floors under Robert de Torigny's rooms contain the porter's lodging and, on the ground floor, two dungeons known as "the two twins". The porter's lodging is adjacent to the monastery entrance, comprised of two round arches set above a broken arch. This small room has been thoroughly modified in the course of

Robert de Torigny's apartments and the entrance to the monastery in the 12th century.

St. Stephen's chapel and the monks' ossuary with the large wheel.

the centuries.
Two holes in the pavement provided the only access to the two twins. The porter-monk was therefore also the prison guard. The dungeon and its history is surrounded by a whole series of melancholy legends. Actually they were built by Robert de Torigny when, as part of his reorganization of the management of the monastery's holdings, he decided to exercise directly the rights of justice over the lands under his control. The prisoners of the "ancien regime" were not, as is frequently stated or written, closed in these two dungeons. At most they were used as disciplinary prisons while the entire abbey, in particular the monks' lodgings, were turned into prisons in modern times.

THE SOUTHERN BUILDINGS

Robert de Torigny had a series of large buildings constructed along the nave on the south side, the most important of which collapsed in 1818. This was the hostelry where noble pilgrims stayed, and on the floor below, a new infirmary for the monks. This building collapsed in 1818.

CHAPELLE SAINT-ETIENNE

The infirmary opened on a chapel which is still extant, although poorly restored. Dedicated to St. Stephen, the chapel served for the wakes of the monks when they died. It is attached to a wall built in the 11th century to defend the monastery and rebuilt at various times during the 13th century.

THE OSSUARY AND THE LARGE WHEEL

The cemetery of the monks seems to have been laid out below the south

wall of the nave of the abbey church as early as the 11th century. On the site Robert de Torigny had an ossuary built, composed of four large arches, of which only one still stands full height for the other three were lowered to support the upper flights of the great abbey staircase. In the 19th century the elevator which served to carry supplies to the prison was installed between two of these arches. What it actually is, is a slide-way consisting of a large wheel which was turned by men who walked on the inside. A rope was thus wound around the axis and pulled a cart up the access ramp to be seen along the south side of the abbey. Lifts of this kind were already known to the ancient Romans and were widely used throughout the Middle Ages. They were the principal lifting machines in the construction yards for the cathedrals. They are often depicted in medieval illuminations and it is known for certain that a lift of this type was used in the 12th century in the wine cellars of the guest house. Another one was installed in the 13th century in the wine cellar of the *Merveille*.

MONASTIC LIFE

Under the abbacy of Robert de Torigny the abbey of Mont-Saint-Michel reached its zenith. At the time the monastery housed sixty monks. The exemplary management of the abbot made it possible to provide a material well-being despite the high costs of the construction work initiated at the time. It was also one of those moments in which the regularity of monastic life seems to have been respected and in which the spirituality of the Mont could be cited as an example.
The production of the scriptorium, even more than the architecture, testifies to the prosperity enjoyed by the monastery. In the 11th century the copyists of Mont-Saint-Michel had already proved their exceptional qualities. Under the administration of Robert de Torigny the library was enriched by about a hundred books, including the cartulary famous for its illustrations. Traditionally, numerous books are ascribed to Robert himself, but actually we know of only one, moderately interesting, chronicle by him.
The illustrious abbot of a powerful monastery, Robert de Torigny played an important role in politics. Very close to Henry II Plantagenet, duke of Normandy and king of England, he received a double pilgrimage in Mont-Saint-Michel during which Henry met the king of France Louis VII.

Monk offering a manuscript to the Archangel Michael - after 966 - Municipal Library of Avranches, MS 50.

◀ *The slide lift of medieval type installed in the 19th century.*

THE MERVEILLE

In 1066 the duke of Normandy also became king of England. The duchy now passed into the hands of the counts of Anjou, the Plantagenets, and when one of them, Henry II, married Eleanor of Aquitaine, new

Dispute between St. Augustine and the Manichaean heretic Faustus - mid-11th century - Municipal Library of Avranches, MS 90.

and farflung possessions were added to his realm. King of the British Isles, Henry II with his holdings on the continent found himself in the position of vassal to a king who was infinitely less powerful. This degenerated into a long conflict that lasted for all of the 12th century.

The Plantagenet empire collapsed at the dawning of the 13th century when the king of France, Philippe Auguste, conquered Normandy at the end of a lightning campaign carried out in 1204. In the course of the campaign a troop of Bretons, allies of the king of France, set fire to Mont-Saint-Michel.

The damage inflicted seems to have been heavy, above all on the north side, where a large building, constructed in the previous century by the abbot Roger II, was engulfed in flames. The lack of funds and the discord which existed between the monks and their abbot, Jourdain, considerably delayed reconstruction. This situation lasted until 1211, the year in which Philippe Auguste, who succeeded the dukes of Normandy as protector of the community of monks, made them an important donation. The following year the abbot Jourdain died. His successor, Raoul des Isles, could now begin the construction of a new monastery on the foundations of the walls that were still standing at the foot of the building which had burned down in 1204.

Three buildings were planned, each with three floors. Thanks to the experience gained in those glorious Benedictine centuries which had just come to an end, the architect was perfectly acquainted with the needs of the community and the types of space required by the various activities of the monks. Moreover, the new construction methods — which we call Gothic — perfected in over half a century in the construction yards of the cathedrals, made it possible to realize the most daring projects.

Two of the three buildings planned were completed in barely seventeen years, from 1211 to 1228. They form what is known as the **Merveille.** The difficulties raised in constructing a complex like this on the slope of a rock stimulated the architect's genius to invent technical solutions which helped create the diversified spatial entities which best corresponded to the various moments of monastic life. The six rooms of the **Merveille**, which taken together form an almost ideal monastery, comprise a truly exceptional lesson in architecture.

The third building originally planned was never realized. The 13th century, in fact, marks an important turning point in the spiritual history of the Middle Ages and, under the impulse of St. Francis of Assisi, the most brilliant monks turned to the mendicant orders and went to preach in the cities among the poor. The regular life in the Benedictine cloisters was no longer the same. The fact that the construction yards of the Merveille were abandoned clearly testifies to this evolution.

The north facade of the Merveille which Victor Hugo called the most beautiful wall in the world.

THE EASTERN BUILDING OF THE MERVEILLE

The eastern building of the **Merveille** is like a series of dining rooms set one over the other: at the top the **refectory** of the monks; below this the **Salle des Hôtes** (or guest room); on the ground floor the **almonry**. A kitchen was installed next to the monks' refectory.
This superposition recalls the hierarchy of medieval society described in the 11th century by Bishop Adalberon de Laon. A social hierarchy corresponds to each room: those who pray eat in the refectory; those who fight, the nobles, were received in the **Salle des Hôtes**; the poor are assisted in the almonry. The building is an image of society as imagined by the ecclesiastics of the Middle Ages. But medieval reality, which was much more complex, found it difficult if not impossible to adapt itself to this scheme and, in practice, various adaptations were inevitable.
As was the case with the western building, the height of the construction and the limited space available on the rock forced the builders to respect a series of rigorous technical imperatives. The refectory was covered by plastered woodwork, the guest room with ribbed cross vaulting and the almonry with groin vaults.
Various signs would seem to indicate that the almonry, as a whole, was a room in Roger II's building that had been spared in the fire of 1204. Similarly the eave walls of the **Salle des Hôtes**, like those of the **Salle des Chevaliers**, could have been preserved and then reused in building the **Merveille**. If this were the case, it would help explain the rapidity with which this outstanding monument was built.

The superposed rooms of the refectory, the Salle des Hôtes and the almonry reflect the social hierarchy of medieval society.

THE WESTERN BUILDING OF THE MERVEILLE

From top to bottom the western building of the Merveille is comprised of the **cloister**, the work-room normally known as the **Salle des Chevaliers**, and the **cellar**.
Each level was conceived in function of a series of rigid technical imperatives: great lightness was necessary at the top and this is proved by the construction of the cloister; underneath, the **Salle des Chevaliers** had to be solid and vaulted in stone to support the cloister; the main problem was that of supporting the weight of the whole structure. Each therefore has a different type of vault: wood on the upper level, ogive cross vaulting on the intermediate level, heavy cross vaults on the ground floor.
The superposition of these rooms also in part corresponds to a hierarchy comprised of the spiritual — the cloister is ideally a place for meditation; the intellectual — in the scriptorium the monks dedicated themselves to study; and the material — in the cellar all kinds of supplies were preserved.
The western building seems to have been built after the eastern building: the sculpture on the upper floors is very deep-cut and creates vibrant contrasts of light and dark. These characteristics are typically Norman in style and mark the years after 1220.
In building the two rooms on the lower floors the architect apparently used a considerable part of what was left of the building of Roger II that had been gutted by fire in 1204. The walls of the cellar and the **Salle des Chevaliers** in fact bear numerous vestiges of the disposition of the Romanesque monastery.

The cloister in the western building which lies above the Salle des Chevaliers and the cellar underneath.

THE MONKS' REFECTORY

The refectory which crowns the eastern building of the **Merveille** constitutes, from the point of view of volumes, one of the most remarkable expressions of all European architecture. Covered by a plastered barrel vault, extremely wide, and scanned in all its length by a series of small columns, full of light even though no sources of light are visible on the sides, the room is awe-inspiring.
The refectory seems made to measure for a community which gathered together here for its meals, presided over by the abbot, in a silence broken only by the reading of an edifying text that served to inspire collective meditation. In the Benedictine rule, the meal is a spiritual as well as material activity: the monk nourishes his soul together with his body.
For this moment that played so essential a role in monastic life, the architect conceived of an imposing space in which the longitudinal axis carries the eye naturally towards the place reserved for the abbot.
The spatial entity seems to be closed, yet surprisingly luminous, for the light penetrates through tall narrow windows set in great number between the inner buttresses which form the wall and conceal the openings of the windows, deepset as they are.
This enclosed space is that of the great Romanesque naves; the light that flows in is that of the Gothic cathedrals. The Romanesque style distinguishes the most important Benedictine structures. Light occupies a fundamental place in the spirituality of the 13th century. In this sense the refectory is a sort of synthesis between the continuity of monastic life and its adaptation to the times.
Within this space, under this light, the acoustics are astonishing. In this hall dedicated to silence, the least sound is amplified and distorted by the echoes. Despite this, from his lectern, but only from there, the reader,

General view of the monks' refectory: a Romanesque space with Gothic light.

Various details of the decoration of the corner supports in the cloister, in stone from Caen. Facing page: the cloister and the west facade of the refectory.

without raising his voice, could be heard by all the monks.
Perfectly conceived for its purpose, the room also represents an undeniable technical feat. The wall which consists of thick buttresses connected to each other with exterior arches at the impost level ensures a perfect resistance to the load-bearing wooden roof. At the same time, the weight is discharged onto the wall of the floor below, which makes it possible to cover the **Salle des Hôtes** underneath with a stone vault without having to reinforce it with flying buttresses. The equilibrium of the refectory thus contributes to the stability of the entire building.
The two problems faced by the architect who was called in to build a solid structure in which the community could also live well thus found a single solution. Technical skill at the service of the monastic idea: this is what makes this such an outstanding room.

THE CLOISTER

Even though it is at the top of the abbey buildings and not at their center, and despite the objective difficulties provided by the absence of a level ground, the cloister which crowns the **Merveille** has conserved the form and functions of the cloisters to be found in all other monasteries. But a few subtle differences set it apart and turn it into a symbolic representation of an ideal monastic life.
As in the other abbeys, it is above all a sort of communications center inherited from the atrium of the Roman villa, providing access to all the essential rooms: to the east, the refectory and the kitchens, no longer extant, opened onto the cloister; to the south, one door led to the church and another one to the dormitory; to the west, the three traditional apertures must have opened into the chapter hall that was never built, and a small door led to the archives. Only the north gallery, in the direction of the ocean, was not meant to serve as a way of communication with other rooms: the principal functions of monastic life, except for work and reception, were thus distributed around the cloister. A passageway, the cloister was also, as in all the other monasteries, the space set aside for the monk's personal meditation. Paradoxically, this symbolic center of the Benedictine abbey, the very essence of which was the community life that St. Benedict considered the only truly monastic way of life, is the only space in which the individual is more important than the community. The columns are as tall as a man and spaced a shoulder's width from each other. This difference in scale compared to the other rooms is all the more striking in view of the fact that truly imposing spaces must be crossed before arriving at the cloister. The impression of weightlessness aroused by the cloister as a whole is thus accen-

The galleries and the garden of the cloister.

tuated.
The purely physical need to make the cloister, which rests on the vaults of another room, as light as possible explains the airy quality which never fails to take the visitor's breath away. It was impossible, at the top of the Merveille, to cover the portico with stone vaults and to make use of columns and buttresses. The covering therefore had to be of wood and the plastered barrel vault in wood provides the galleries with their astounding perspective. The weight and thrust of the framework are sustained externally by thick solid granite walls, decorated with blind arcading, and inside by the double arcade, set slightly askew, with its two overlapping rows of pointed arches. These authentic small ogive cross vaults in between carried on the acutely pointed arches hollow out the wall and ensure the triangulation which provides the whole with a perfect stability.
Unusual esthetic effects combine with the physical advantages of this type of architecture. The unbroken continuity in the rhythm of the supports and the absence of the solid masonry at the corners permit the eye to move unhindered and at the same time assures an absolute transparency towards the center of the cloister. Indeed, closed off from the outside more than any other, the cloister is extraordinarily open towards the inside. It represents the life the monk leads in the cloistered monastery, absorbed in his meditation. His hope must be that of meriting heaven, which, as it should be, is omnipresent in this space. The cloister is in fact so placed that no other building rises higher and the slope of the roof reaches directly towards the sky, which penetrates the central space and draws our attention upwards. This symbolic aspect turns a place of meditation into a subject for meditation.
Unfortunately later restorations have considerably changed the character of the cloister. Practically all the columns, once made of limestone imported from England, were replaced in 1878. The change in material also meant a change in color and in spirit. Even more lamentable is the opening of the three apertures which were originally meant to lead to the chapter hall. Walled up until the 19th century, they now transform the cloister into a belvedere, drawing our attention to the sand and sea rather than the sky as had been the architect's intention. The creation of a garden at

the center of the cloister would have been impossible before modern methods of waterproofing were perfected. This addition is due to Y. M. Froidevaux, an architect charged with the preservation of historical monuments, whose work left a deep mark on Mont-Saint-Michel in the latter part of the 19th century.
The restoration of the sculpture was not as radical and keeps faith with the spirit of the cloister where the wall in stone from Caen, above the small columns, is abundantly covered with sculpture. All the spandrels between the arches are filled with plant elements. It is a mirror of nature, a recurrent theme in 13th-century Gothic art, here betraying marked regional features. The Norman school was at its zenith when the cloister was built. It was characterized by a particularly deep carving, and by the fact that the decorative elements invaded the wall, which tended to vanish from sight. In Mont-Saint-Michel the decorative elements project from the plane of the wall, all carved in depth with a marked play of dark and light. The sculptors may be the three figures, don Garin, master Pierre and master Roger, represented in the south gallery. The only other figures in the decoration are a vintner in front of the refectory and, above all, four religious figures facing the openings which were to lead to the chapter hall. They depict St. Aubert, the founder, Christ on the Cross, Christ in Majesty and, oddly enough, St. Francis of Assisi. Under the figure of Francis a scroll which disappeared in the revolution noted that the cloister had been completed in the year the saint was canonized, 1228. The representation of St. Francis is important on two counts: one is that this is one of the oldest portraits of the 'Poverello' who died in 1226, the other is that the figure is right opposite the three openings which marked the abandonment of the construction yard of the Merveille. This coincidence testifies to the simultaneous birth of a new religious feeling in the 13th century, embodied in the mendicant orders, and the decline of the Benedictines, who give up constructing buildings of spiritual vocation and shortly thereafter begin to build abbeys which are veritable temporal palaces.
The cloister of the Merveille, a major example of architecture, bearer of ideas that seem eternal, however still falls into a well-defined historical perspective.

Verticality characterizes the columns and windows of the Salle des Hôtes.

SALLE DES HÔTES

Although the area covered by the Salle des Hotês is the same as that of the monks' refectory which it supports, it looks completely different. While the latter induces meditation, the former seems dedicated to ease. There is something festive about the atmosphere, due in part to the slender columns, in part to the extremely tall windows which consist of narrow two-light openings, all forming a sheaf of vertical lines. The only decorative element still extant, the sculptured capitals, contribute to this search for verticality. In fact from the bell of the capital foliage echoes the movement of the quadripartite ribbed vaults, avoiding an interruption in the ascending lines of the architecture. More than anything else, the room must be envisioned as richly decorated, with frescoed vaulting, painted wooden paneling or tapestries lining the walls, tile pavements with the coats of arms of France and Castille, in honor of the king and queen, Louis VIII and Blanche of Castille. Some consider this room, the first truly Gothic work in Mont-Saint-Michel, a French importation. Apart from the fact that it is anterior to similar halls on the Ile de France,

The enormous fireplaces in the Salle des Hôtes comprised "the kitchens" for the pilgrims.

Royaumont, Saint-Martin-des-Champs or Noyon, the premises for the Norman Gothic school — hexagonal bases and capitals with a round abacus — are to be found here.
The west wall is completely taken up by two immense fireplaces which allowed the guests to prepare their own food. Pilgrims could thus arrive at any time and get a meal without disturbing the preparations for the repast of the monks whose religious duties came first.
This is probably the room in which the kings of France, from St. Louis to Henry III, were received when they came on pilgrimage to Mont-Saint-Michel. We know from the agreement on its use, stipulated in 1258 between the monks and the abbot Richard Turstin, that here "the friends and relatives of the friends of the monks" were received. These words, whose meaning in medieval terminology is precise and indicates all those who have made a large donation to the abbey, allows us to presume that, thanks to the interplay of lineages, all the nobility were admitted to this hostelry, which replaced the one built by Robert de Torigny a century earlier at the other end of the monastery.

The Salle des Chevaliers, an outstanding example of Norman Gothic architecture.

SALLE DES CHEVALIERS

Situated under the cloister, the Salle des Chevaliers is on the second level of the Merveille. Built shortly after the Salle des Hôtes, in the same building, with the same material — granite — and with the same technique — ogive cross vaulting — the room nevertheless looks completely different.

And the concept is actually quite different: four aisles instead of two, separated by three rows of columns with the row furthest south, on the opposite side of the fireplaces, resting directly on the rock. Upon entering, the room immediately appears very spacious and large. But unlike the hospice where a single glance tells all, it seems broken up, almost obstructed by the many columns. Their form helps create a sense of balance. Far from being slender vertical arrows shooting upwards towards the vaults, they provide a sense of solidity, of confidence, that is inspired by their rather squat proportions and the fact that they are built of low drums with thick separating joints.
The shape of the windows also contributes to this search for balance. Round where possible, otherwise with round-headed arches, the openings on the north wall were meant to trans-

Another view of the Salle des Chevaliers.

mit a diffused regulated light. In reality however an immense opening in the west wall, originally meant to lead to a room that was never built, doubtlessly the library, which would have supported the chapter hall, floods the room with light and creates an atmosphere completely unlike that planned by the architect.
A regular even light is one of the essential requisites for a scriptorium. And it was here that from the 13th century on the monks busied themselves with copying and illuminating their books. Actually as early as the 12th century the growing number of universities had led to the opening of numerous book stalls so that a circuit of production and distribution of manuscripts was created outside the abbeys. The monks themselves acquired books there and their scriptorium was, without doubt, given the date of its construction, more a place of study than of copying.
The two fireplaces which permitted the monks to take the chill off their fingers during the day and to warm themselves after the night office of the matins were situated far from each other, to heat a larger surface. The hood is supported by two long granite brackets which permitted the heat to radiate better. Behind the chimneys are the latrines, preceded by small galleries that overlook the bay.

THE ALMONRY

Situated under the Salle des Hôtes, which supports the monks' refectory, the almonry is the only room preserved intact when the buildings dating to the first quarter of the 12th century were destroyed by fire in 1204. This Romanesque room is of an absolute simplicity. No sculpture decorates the capitals with their square abacus, no ribs enrich the surface of the groin vaults where only the corbels mark the springing of the vaults.
No trace remains of the paintings which decorated the walls, and the aspect of the almonry is austere. But there is an aura of restrained power to the interior which must have been reassuring for those who were received here.
The function of the room was reception. Not the reception of the mighty who were offered the pomp of the Salle des Hôtes, but that which St. Benedict asked be reserved for the poor, and which was to be of the best kind. Actually it seems unlikely that all the pilgrims could have been received in the almonry. It was rather the place where meals were distributed to the poor, in conditions which varied with the times. The existence of a silent butler between the refectory and this room, in the northeast corner,

would seem to indicate that, at the time it was built, the custom prevailed that, as at Cluny, the meals the monks did not eat on fast days were distributed to the poor.

THE CELLAR

The supplies needed by the monks and their guests were stored in the cellar on the ground floor of the western building of the Merveille. Architectural esthetics or decoration were unnecessary in a strictly utilitarian space like this.
What was needed to support the weight of the upper floors, that is the cloister and the Salle des Chevaliers, was a solid structure. The square piers of the cellar fulfill this requirement, without futile attempts at esthetics. There is not even a capital. At the top of each pier a simple impost block suffices to receive the vaults where the groins are not even stressed by ribs. In this cellar it is difficult to distinguish exactly what is 13th century and what is left of the building that was burned in 1204.
There is no doubt that some of the masonry, reddened and swollen, went through fire. Added to this are the vestiges of a floor or level that was planned but never completely carried out. This would explain the difference between the three aisles and the strange shape of the one on the north where the internal buttresses occupy all but a narrow corridor. An opening in the north wall let in the supplies that were hoisted up with the aid of a large wheel. Outside, a ramp descended to the beach, near the fountain of St. Aubert.

◀ The almonry has a copy of the model of the Mont, made in 1701 and now in the Model Museum.

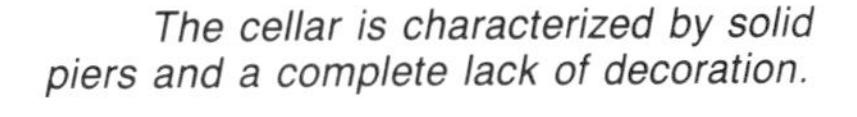

The cellar is characterized by solid piers and a complete lack of decoration.

THE GUARD ROOM

Formerly overlooking the ocean, towards the Norman coast of Genêts from which the greatest number of pilgrims and most of the supplies arrived, this entrance was moved to the southeast, near the almonry, after the construction of the Merveille.
Entrance into the monastery is through the guard room, after having climbed stairs so steep they were called **le Gouffe** (the Abyss). This room follows the slope of the rock, so that the pavement is articulated in three levels and ogive cross vaults above are at different heights.
Rather than a self-sufficient room, it seems more like a fragment of the guard walk leading to the sanctuary that has been enlarged and roofed over. Originally rectangular, it was shortened in the 15th century with masonry that served as a foundation for the Gothic apse of the abbey church. An opening let into the rock during restoration work provides a glimpse of the vault that continues inside the wall.
A doorway, on the east, opens on the courtyard of the Merveille and provides access to the almonry. The **great interior staircase** begins on the other side.
This monumental work, which leads up to the abbey church, is actually a street within the monastery. Squeezed between the abbey lodgings on the south and the foundations of the church on the north, in certain points the staircase almost seems to be a cliff that must be climbed to reach the final goal of the pilgrimage.
Like all the entrances to the abbey it was strongly defended. Halfway up, traces of a portcullis are still to be seen, and it was protected by two fortified bridges. At the top, the staircase terminates on the terrace of Saut-Gautier, from which a magnificent view of the landscape to the south and the polders is to be had.

The guard room, with the three levels of paving which follow the slope of the rock, and the Grand Degré, the internal stairway which leads to the abbey church.

BELLE-CHAISE AND THE ABBOT'S LODGINGS

In the 11th century a small room at the west end of the monastery served as an office for managing the monastery property. By the 13th century the importance of temporal power had grown enormously, both in the real world and as far as the community and the abbot were concerned. This was why Richard Turstin had a new room built under the guard's room that was meant to house the court that administered justice in the name of the owner of the land who was the abbot. Know as Belle-Chaise, a name it received after Pierre Le Roy, abbot in the 14th century, had installed a sumptuous chair there, the room is lighted by a row of tall vertical windows which recall those of the refectory.

The building of the Belle-Chaise marks the beginning of an enormous construction yard which was to completely alter the southern facade of Mont-Saint-Michel into its present aspect. Later the abbot Pierre Le Roy had a tower built as lodging for the garrison, baptized with his own name as tour Perrine, and then the residence of the bailiff where his proxy lived. His own lodgings were built on the other side. The rift between the abbot, absorbed in his official role of head of administrative services which were continually increasing in importance, and the rest of the community grew ever wider. A result of this state of affairs was that from the second half of the 13th century on, the only outstanding work, apart from the reconstruction of the choir after the Hundred Years War, was concerned with the bishop's palace. At present these apartments are in part occupied by the community of monks, and in part by the offices involved in the preservation of the monument.

The Belle-Chaise where the bishop's court met and the abbey lodgings seen from the south.

THE HUNDRED YEARS WAR

A true image of the Middle Ages, Mont-Saint-Michel also reflects its crises. At the end of the 13th century, the abbey already seemed to have outlived its scope. The transferral of the construction yards from the chapter hall to the abbot's apartments are a sign of the shift in interest of the monastery from the spiritual to the temporal.
In the middle of the 14th century, with the beginning of the war between France and England, the crisis deepened. The many truces between one military campaign operation and the next, essentially simply furnished an opportunity to prepare for the next bout. The end of the 14th century was marked by the construction of the defenses nearest the sanctuary.
The present entry to the monastery dates to this period. Before the guard room, flanking the staircase of le Gouffre, the steepness of which was also an integral part of the defenses, the **two towers of the Châtelet** embody a period in which the art of fortification and the esthetic aspect went hand in hand. The alternating use of courses of grey and pink granite reflects a concept of war which took into consideration the artistic value of the sanctuary.
Below the Châtelet, which dominates from on high, an ensemble of walls, barbicans and long flights of stairs is joined to the fortifications built beginning in the 13th century to the northeast of Mont-Saint-Michel. An attacker who had managed to penetrate the village would then have found himself confronted with a defensive system which would have stopped him from taking the sanctuary dedicated to the archangel Michael, patron saint of the King of France.
With Agincourt, still another defeat in which the French cavalry was massacred, the war took a new turn. In 1420 the treaty of Troyes recognized the defeat of the French. And as if that were not enough, in 1421 the vaults of the choir of the abbey church collapsed.

The round towers of the Châtelet and the fortifications immediately below.

THE FLAMBOYANT GOTHIC CHOIR

As long as the war lasted, reconstruction was obviously out of the question. Not until after the victory could plans for building a new choir be set in motion.

The abbot at the time was Guillaume d'Estouteville, brother of the captain of Mont-Saint-Michel, and above all, bishop of Rouen, who loved luxury and who maintained close ties with the king and the pope. It was not enough for this grand prelate simply to repair the damages suffered by the abbey church, all of four centuries old. There was no question but that a completely new church should be built, in the style of the times, flamboyant Gothic.

Construction began with the new choir. To support the weight, the **crypte des gros Piliers** (crypt of the large piers) was built. The enormous cylindrical columns are doubtless a simple encasing of the Romanesque supports which still exist behind the granite facing. Unlike its Romanesque predecessor, this crypt was no longer meant to be a sacred place, but an example of architectural virtuosity and material force.

Above the crypt which supports it, the **choir** of the new church was the result of the developments that had taken place in medieval architecture.

Gothic techniques, used with consummate skill, go almost unnoticed in the search for special effects, lines and light. The key word for this architecture might be 'verticality'. From the base of the columns to the keystones in the vault, the line seems to move in one great sweep, leading the eye towards the sky whose presence is felt behind the windows which replace the walls in the upper parts of the choir. Nothing impedes the light from entering the sanctuary.

The molding of the columns which almost seems to transform them into jets of water, the disappearance of the vertical line of the capitals, the light which comes in from the open window behind the columns at the level of the triforium all play a role in the dilation of the architectural space.

The flamboyant Gothic choir is supported by the Crypte des Gros-Piliers.

Outside, the choir almost seems set into the bezel of its counter-revetments. To counter the thrust of the flying arches on the buttresses, these have been submerged in pinnacles, multiple spires decorated with crockets. The sobriety of the interior, where the richness is created by the purity of simple lines, is countered by the chasing of the exterior. The **'lace stair'**, which owes its name to the carving of the granite banisters, seems the apotheosis of this daring. Resting on a flying buttress, to the south of the choir, it leads directly to the roof in the midst of the forest of spires, more than a hundred meters above the strand. In the aura of enthusiasm in the wake of the victory, a grandiose project took shape. As things returned to normality, the impetus died down. Begun in 1450, the choir was not finished until 1521. The Middle Ages had by then come to an end. The spiritual, intellectual and cultural centers of the society had shifted to the towns, or near the sumptuous dwellings the king and his relatives had built for themselves on the banks of the Loire. The termination of what for seventy years the monks had defined 'le grand oeuvre' was abandoned and the choir in flamboyant Gothic style remained forever set against the Romanesque transept, without any transition between the two. This juxtaposition of two important periods and two styles of architecture provides us with a comparison of two sensibilities and two mentalities.

The spires of the Gothic choir, the interior and a bas-relief in the north transept depicting the Four Evangelists.

The neoclassic facade of the church seen from the west platform.

THE MONT IN MODERN TIMES

With the advent of the Renaissance, a period of lethargy began for Mont-Saint-Michel, defined by some as decadence. A new society means a new spirituality and a new mentality. In the 16th century the more dynamic wing of monasticism no longer withdrew from the world to dedicate itself completely to a life of contemplation but its new mission — with the Jesuits — was that of forming the new elite. The number of monks in Mont-Saint-Michel dwindled, forced as they were to share their revenue, most of which the commendatory abbot nominated by the king of France dilapidated far from the monastery walls.
Despite the ever greater signs of decline, a few attempts to beautify the sanctuary were still made in the 16th century as witnessed by a few fragments of a choir screen with the four evangelists depicted in the most important reliefs. But the unrelenting state of war — the war against the people of a foreign country, the English, had been replaced by a civil war against the Protestants - was not particularly favorable to monastic life. Stronghold of the league, in other words the front-line Catholics, in the second half of the century Mont-Saint-Michel was repeatedly attacked by the Huguenots led by Montgommery. Betrayal followed betrayal on the summit of this small rock.
In the 17th century, with peace once more reigning, the Benedictine monks of the congregation of Saint-Maur took over the reins of Mont-Saint-Michel. They arrived in 1622 and settled in the buildings of the **Merveille** in 1629. These monks greatly furthered the activity of historical research which characterized their congregation, giving rise to the expression 'a Benedictine labor'. The histories of Mont-Saint-Michel compiled by these Maurist monks comprise our principle documentary source after the bombing of Saint-Lô in 1944 completely destroyed the archives of the abbey.
The lack of financial means, in a period when the concept of preservation of the patrimony did not yet exist, was the reason behind most of the damage done to the buildings. For example, in 1776 when the facade and the first three bays of the nave threa Stened to collapse at the risk of the Romanesque buildings below, it was decided then and there to demolish everything that was unstable, destroying about half the nave. A new facade was thus built. Its classic proportions succeed only in expressing the miserable condition of a monastery in decline. The imitation Romanesque capitals are perhaps the only original touch and they herald the neo-Romanesque style which became popular a century later.
The French Revolution brought an end to this long agony. The few monks who still lived there left the monastery. The abbey of Mont-Saint-Michel, by now an enormous empty shell, was ready to be used for whatever fate should have in store.

THE MONT, STATE PRISON

In the 15th century under the reign of Louis XI the monastery of Mont-Saint-Michel had already served as a prison. It had the earned the sinister name of 'Bastille of the Seas' and was where political adversaries of the monarch and the 'exiled' agitators were housed, often in appalling conditions.
It is no wonder therefore that in 1792 the monument followed its calling as penitentiary. The priests who objected to the civil constitution of the clergy were the first successors of those bearing arbitrary warrants of imprisonments who had been imprisoned or exiled there. It was then the turn of the Vendeans and the Chouans (Breton loyalist insurgents), closely followed by the republicans and common criminals.
Mont-Saint-Michel was to remain a state prison until 1863. Every now and then the penitentiary administration realized how important the monument was and restoration was begun, as after the fire which destroyed the abbey church in 1834. This did not however prevent Robert de Torigny's hostelry from collapsing in 1818.
In order to house 600 prisoners, it was necessary to readapt the rooms, dividing and transforming them. At this time the advent of Romanticism and the appearance of the concept of 'historical monument' played essential roles in drawing the attention of the world to the outstanding importance of this unique monument.
The problem of what Mont-Saint-Michel should be used for was once more raised in 1863 when the central penitentiary was closed. For ten years the buildings again housed a community of monks who were however unable to cope with the gigantic restoration works which had become indispensable. At this point only the State was capable of taking on the preservation of Mont-Saint-Michel, which it did in 1874 through the Department of Fine Arts.

The neo-Romanesque bell tower of the abbey and the neo-Gothic spire.

The stone entrance stairway on the south side of the abbey. Inside is the large wheel.

THE RESTORATION

The various head architects of historical monuments who throughout the years were charged with the restoration of Mont-Saint-Michel all left their mark on the building entrusted to them, reflecting the evolution of the attitude to medieval architecture as well as its interpretation and the theory of restoration.
Walls were reinforced pretty much everywhere and intonaco and roofs were redone. This continuous work of restoration saved the abbey and the ramparts from certain death and are what gave the Mont its present aspect. The state in which the crossing and the bell tower were in was so critical that between 1892 and 1897 Victor Petitgrand had to rebuild them from scratch. The result was the neo-Romanesque bell tower and the neo-Gothic spire, whose sharp point topped by a gilded statue of the archangel has become a symbol of the eternal crowning of Mont-Saint-Michel. The image known the world over is actually a creation of the *Belle Epoque*, and as such it must be regarded.
Nowadays even the restorations are being restored. Mont-Saint-Michel seems to be destined to be an eternal construction yard.

THE RAMPARTS

The abbey's millenary history, the prestige of the church and its buildings, its site on top of the rock, reflecting the supremacy of spiritual things in medieval society — all this has always overshadowed the military architecture of Mont-Saint-Michel.
The ramparts that encircle the rock nevertheless represent an unusual complex of architecture. Front-line in the defense of the abbey but at the same time dominated, and therefore protected, by it, the ramparts surround the entire village. The structure of Mont-Saint-Michel is typical of the medieval signorias: the abbey is the residence of the lord, the keep. At the base of this citadel lie the more immediate defenses, the Châtelet and the barbican. Beyond this, the city walls, which would be the lower court were this an ordinary castle.
The earliest mention of fortifications around the sanctuary of the archangel dates to the 10th century. Richard I, who installed the Benedictine monks there in 966, apparently provided them with funds for the construction of a circle of walls which was probably a simple wooden palisade, of which no trace remains.
The military vocation of the Mont made its appearance at the end of the

General view of Mont-Saint-Michel from the east.

The Tour du Nord.

The curtain wall between the Tour du Nord and the Tour Boucle.

Machicolations of the bastion seen from the Tour Boucle.

11th century: Henri, son of William the Conqueror, who was then to become duke of Normandy and king of England as Henry I Beauclerc, was unsuccessfully besieged by his two brothers in 1091. Nor did the Bretons, led by Guy de Thouars, succeed in penetrating the Mont in 1204. Since it was unthinkable to leave a fortress of this sort behind them as they continued their campaign through Normandy, they set fire to it and were thus indirectly responsible for the construction of the Merveille.

These two events by themselves suffice to prove the existence of a system of defenses way before the oldest extant parts of the ramparts, the ones closest to the abbey, were built. At its foot, the **tour Claudine**, which now serves as entrance to the northern gardens, marks the beginning of the circuit of city walls, at the point in which it joins the barbican of the Châtelet. A curtain wall begins here, upon which the guard walk of the ramparts passes and from which there is a magnificent view over the bay, particularly the eastern part. Flanked by imposing towers, these ramparts continue as far as the north tower, the highest in the circuit, and then gradually descend along the slope of the rock. The guard walk is then replaced by a staircase, at the foot of which the lay-out of the fortifications built in the 13th century distinguishes itself from those which date to the Hundred Years War. The first circle of walls must have continued through where the village now is, climbing up the south side of the abbey and probably passing in the point where the parish church now stands.

All of the fortifications which were at sea level, from the **tour Boucle** to the **King's Gate**, were built between 1417 and 1420 by the abbot Robert Jolivet, whose coat of arms is carved in the escutcheon held by the stone figure of a lion set in a niche.

At this point in the war, when the French cavalry was defeated by the English archers, the abbot of Mont-Saint-Michel, who was nominated captain of the place by the king of France, did all he could to protect the sanctuary of the archangel from enemy raids. The quality of his interventions is demonstrated in a strange way. A 'Legaliste', Robert Jolivet accepted the treaty of Troyes and in 1420 passed to the English side. Here his influence was such that he was charged with taking the Mont from the handful of Knights — 119 according to tradition — who, gathered around Louis d'Estouteville, incarnated the resistence of the French nation which was then in its birth throes.

The siege of Mont-Saint-Michel lasted from 1420 to 1450, with only brief interruptions. There were two crucial moments in which the English attempted to conquer the rock. In 1425 there was a complete blockade, both on land and sea. The sailors of Saint-Malo succeeded in loosening the vice which was closing in on Mont-Saint-Michel. In 1434 the English launched a particularly violent attack, preced-

The Tour Boucle.

The Demi-Lune and the Tour Boucle.

The coat-of-arms of Robert Jolivet, abbot of the Mont, who built the ramparts.

ed by an intense artillery bombardment which permitted them to open a breach in the ramparts. A victorious sally of the French knights put them to flight.
The periods of truce were used to reinforce the fortifications. Louis d'Estouteville had the **tour Boucle** built, a spur with ramparts, which in the early 15th century heralded the defenses Vauban was to develop two centuries later. Since the history of military architecture is really nothing but the countermeasures taken against the inventions of the assailants, this reveals the rapidity with which military techniques evolved in the Hundred Years War.
The **Demi-Lune**, the **tour Basse**, the **tour de la Liberté**, the **tour de l'Arcade** and the **tour du Roi** mark the

The Tour de la Liberté and the Tour Basse.

The Tour du Roi and the Tour de l'Arcade.

The guard walk and the top of the House of the Arches.

Panorama of the city walls of the Fanils and the Tour Gabriel.

series of walls which move down towards the King's Gate. It is difficult to tell what part dates to Robert Jolivet and what was readapted by Louis d'Estouteville (although we do know that the latter doubled the thickness of at least one part of the ramparts) or what was later restored. Even though it is well preserved, this extraordinary circuit has certainly not been turned to account by the causeway to the Mont, which runs right against the tower of the King and the **Arcade**, lowering the height of the ramparts by several meters. This outstanding fortification which throughout the centuries has resisted attacks of all kinds, is now no more than the setting for an operetta in the precise place where tens of thousands of visitors discover it each year.

The main circuit, which belongs to the village, rises to the abbey in a series of walls that climb up the rock on the south. To protect the entrance to the city — the weak point in the entire fortifications — from the artillery attacks, a boulevard was built in the 15th century to which Gabriel de Puy added an outpost a century later.

ENCEINTE DES FANILS AND THE TOUR GABRIEL

The **Enceinte des Fanils** (walls) protected the storerooms of the abbey situated at the base of the rock, on the western slope, and was dominated by two towers. Nothing but the base remains of that of the **Pêcheurs**, at the foot of the structure built in 1828 as barracks for the prison guards.
In 1524 Gabriel de Puy, military engineer who had built the outpost which defended the entrance to the city, finished the enceinte des Fanils with the **tour Gabriel**. The ramparts were planned with an eye to the latest developments in the field of artillery, as a result of which it is possible to shoot in all directions in the least possible time. In the 18th century, when the military vocation of Mont-Saint-Michel had been superceded, a windmill was set up on the platform of this tower.
In the 19th century a lighthouse was added to act as beacon for navigation of the Couresnon.

The Chapel of Saint Aubert seen from the western terrace.

Isolated by water at high tide, the small **chapel of St. Aubert**, built in the 15th century on an outcropping of the rock, almost looks like a miniature Mont-Saint-Michel. It would be a perfect image but for the fact that it lacks the complete picture of the life of man which makes Mont-Saint-Michel absolutely unique.

All the preoccupations of our medieval forebears, spiritual, intellectual, military or material, are mirrored in the village, its bastions and the abbey.

Mont-Saint-Michel offers unlimited material for meditation — all one has to do is look. It demands to be visited, lived in, 'felt'. There is no end to what can be discovered.

With its wealth of history, shaped by time, Mont-Saint-Michel emerges from its past so that we may discover, above and beyond the stones, the image of humanity, its fears and hopes. Myth that has become reality, it erases the boundaries between the imaginary and the real.